Foundation Paper 1
Financial Accounting Fundamentals

First edition 2002
Third edition January 2004

ISBN 0 7517 1480 1 (Previous edition 0 7517 0116 5)

British Library Cataloguing-in-Publication Data

A catalogue record for this book is available from the British Library

Published by

BPP Professional Education, Aldine House, Aldine Place, London W12 8AW

www.bpp.com

Printed in Great Britain by Ashford Colour Press

Welcome to BPP's CIMA **Passcards**.

- They **save you time**. Important topics are summarised for you.
- They incorporate **diagrams** to kick start your memory.
- They follow the overall **structure** of the BPP Study Texts, but BPP's CIMA **Passcards** are not just a condensed book. Each card has been separately designed for clear presentation. Topics are self contained and can be grasped visually.
- CIMA **Passcards** are **just the right size** for pockets, briefcases and bags.
- CIMA **Passcards focus on the exam** you will be facing.

Run through the complete set of **Passcards** as often as you can during your final revision period. The day before the exam, try to go through the **Passcards** again! You will then be well on your way to passing your exams.

Good luck!

BPP also publishes a Practice & Revision Kit and MCQ cards, which contain lots of questions for you to attempt during your final revision period.

		Page
1	The nature and objectives of accounting	1
2	Preparing accounts: concepts, conventions and regulations	7
3	Assets, liabilities and the accounting equation	15
4	An introduction to final accounts	19
5	Sources, records and the books of prime entry	25
6	Ledger accounting and double entry	33
7	From trial balance to financial statements	39
8	The cost of goods sold, accruals and prepayments	47
9	Discounts, bad debts and provisions	51
10	Accounting for stocks	55
11	Fixed assets - depreciation, revaluation and disposal	61
12	Bank reconciliations	69
13	Control accounts	73
14	Accounting for value added tax	79
15	Accounting for wages and salaries	83
16	Correction of errors. Preparation of final accounts	89
17	The accounts of unincorporated organisations	95

		Page
18	Incomplete records	105
19	Limited companies	113
20	Manufacturing accounts and cash flow statements	123
21	Internal and external audit	133
22	Interpreting company accounts	141

1: The nature and objectives of accounting

Topic List

The purpose of accounting information

Users of accounting information

Management and financial accounting

The main financial statements

This chapter looks at why accounts are prepared.

The role of the accountant and the nature of accounting information help put the rest of the syllabus in context.

A business has a number of functions, the most prominent is to make a profit for the owners

Profit is the excess of income over expenditure

Accounts

Accounting is collecting, recording, summarising and communicating financial information.

Accounts show where money came from and how it has been spent.

Asset

Something valuable which a business owns or has use of

- A factory or warehouse
- Stocks of goods for resale
- Cash

Liability

Something owed to somebody else

- Bank loan
- Amounts owed to suppliers
- Taxation owed to government

Users of accounts

- Managers of the company
- Shareholders of the company
- Trade contacts
- Providers of finance to the company
- Inland Revenue
- Employees of the company
- Financial analysts and advisers
- Government and their agencies
- The public

The larger the business, the greater the interest from various groups of people.

You may be asked in an objective test question to identify the information needs of a user group and how they are satisfied by a set of financial statements

Accountants may qualify with a number of different professional bodies. They may also fulfil a variety of roles within any type of organisation.

Professional bodies

ACCA
CIMA
AAT
ICAEW
CIPFA

Industry and commerce

- Financial managers
- Financial accountants
- Management accountants
- Internal auditors

Public practice

- External audit
- Tax compliance
- Accounts preparation
- Business advice

Public sector

- Trading
- Semi-trading
- Public service

Financial accounting is the preparation of accounting reports for external use. Management accounting is the preparation of accounting reports for internal use.

Financial accounts

- Solely concerned with summarising historical data
- Use same information as management accounts but in a different way
- External users have different interests from management
- Prepared under constraints that do not apply to management accounts

Management accounts

- Detailed information split between departments
- Based on historical information but is forward looking
- Used to prepare forecasts and budgets
- Compare actual performance with budget and take corrective action

Main financial statements

Balance sheet

A list of assets owned by the business and liabilities owed by the business on a particular date

- Total assets = Total liabilities
- Amount invested by owner is **capital**

Profit and loss account

A record of income generated and expenditure incurred over a given period

The financial statements are prepared on an accruals basis

Accruals concept

A sale or purchase is dealt with in the period it is made, even if cash changes hands later than this

2: Preparing accounts: concepts, conventions and regulations

Topic List

Accounting concepts and principles

Costs and values

The regulatory framework

Modern day accounting is based on certain concepts and conventions.

Get to grips with these and you should be well equipped to cope with questions on accounting standards and their strengths and weaknesses.

FRS 18 *Accounting policies* has two accounting concepts which form the bedrock of accounting

Going concern

The business will continue in operational existence for the foreseeable future, and there is no intention to put the company into liquidation or to make drastic cutbacks to the scale of the operation.

Accruals

Revenue and costs must be recognised as they are earned or incurred, not as money is received or paid.

Entity:	the business is an entity distinct from its owners
Money measurement:	accounts deal only with items to which monetary value can be given
Prudence:	where there is uncertainty and alternative procedures or valuations are possible, the one selected should give the most cautious presentation of the entity's position or results
Consistency:	similar items should be accorded similar treatment
Separate value principle:	each component of an asset or liability should be valued separately
Materiality:	only items material in amount or in their nature will affect the true and fair view given by the accounts

Historical cost: transactions are recorded at the amount the business paid to acquire them

Criticisms of historical cost accounting

Historical cost accounting can be misleading for the following reasons.

- Fixed asset values are unrealistic
- Depreciation is inadequate to finance purchase of new assets
- Holding gains on stocks are included in profit
- Profits (or losses) on holdings of net monetary items are not shown
- The true effect of inflation on capital maintenance is not shown
- Comparisons over time are unrealistic

Current purchasing power and current cost accounting

Current purchasing power has the following features:

- Adjusts for general changes in prices
- Not widely accepted

Current cost accounting operates as follows:

- Profit to be calculated after allowing for the effects of price increases specifically in the operating capability of the particular business
- The principal features of CCA are:-
  - Balance sheet – assets stated at 'value to the business'
  - Profit and loss account – holding gains excluded from profit

Influences upon financial accounting

Company law

Form and content of accounts regulated by CA 85. 'True and fair view'.

Accounting concepts and individual judgement

Accounting standards

The ASB produces standards. The UITF and the Review Panel help tackle issues/departures from standards.

GAAP

(Generally accepted accounting practice)

Drawn from:

- Company law
- Accounting standards
- IASs
- The Stock Exchange

International issues

see next page

International influences

The UK must follow EU legislation, by enacting laws to comply with EU directives.

The International Accounting Standards Board: IASs/IFRSs. (The IASC became the IASB in a restructuring during March 2001. Future international standards will be IFRSs.)

The international influence on UK accounting is very important. There is an overall move to harmonise all accounting standards within the EU. All listed companies will need to comply with IASs/IFRSs by 2005.

True and fair view

CA 1985 requires

- The balance sheet must give a true and fair view of the company's affairs at the period end
- The P&L account must give a true and fair view of the profit or loss for the period

↓

There is no definition of 'true and fair'

Standard setting process

FINANCIAL REPORTING COUNCIL
Oversees/sets work programme

ASB

- independent of CCAB
- issues financial reporting standards
- adopted the SSAPs published by predecessor the ASC

UITF

- offshoot of ASB
- tackles urgent matters where normal process too slow
- issues 'abstracts'

REVIEW PANEL

- enforces standards by reviewing companies which fail to comply
- power to apply to courts for revision of accounts

3: Assets, liabilities and the accounting equation

Topic List

The nature of a business

The accounting equation

The business equation

This chapter looks at the fundamental mechanics of financial statements.

The accounting and business equations will help you see why the balance sheet must balance.

Definition

A business is an organisation which sells something, or provides a service, with the objective of making a profit.

A **balance sheet** is a list of all the assets owned and liabilities owed at a particular date

A **profit and loss account** is a record of income generated and expenses incurred over a given period

Non-profit making organisations →

- Charities
- Public sector organisations
- Clubs and associations

The accounting equation

CAPITAL + LIABILITIES = ASSETS

Capital

Investment of funds with the intention of earning a return

Drawings

Amounts withdrawn from the business by the proprietor

The accounting equation is based on the principle that the business is an entity separate from the owner.

The business equation

$$P = I + D - C_i$$

Key

- **P** = profits
- **I** = increase in the business' net assets over a period
- **D** = withdrawal of funds by the owners (drawings)
- **C_i** = increase in capital thanks to an injection of funds by the owners

These two equations are the basis for the balance sheet and the profit and loss account. Understanding these will help you understand the preparation of financial statements.

4: An introduction to final accounts

Topic List

- The balance sheet
- The trading, profit and loss account
- Capital and revenue expenditure

This is an introduction to the main financial statements.

You should be able to reproduce the balance sheet and the profit and loss account formats as well as discuss the main elements of them.

The balance sheet

is a list of assets, liabilities and capital of a business at a given moment

JEDSTER
BALANCE SHEET AS AT 31 AUGUST 20X1

Fixed assets	£	£
Freehold premises		100,000
Fixtures and fittings		16,000
Motor vehicles		18,000
		134,000
Current assets		
Stocks	32,000	
Debtors	1,000	
Cash	800	
	33,800	

Current liabilities		
Bank overdraft	4,000	
Creditors	3,600	
Taxation payable	7,000	
	14,600	
Net current assets		19,200
		153,200
Long-term liabilities		
Loan		(50,000)
Net assets		103,200
Capital		
Capital as at 1 September 20X0		95,200
Profit for the year		16,000
		111,200
Less drawings		(8,000)
Capital as at 31 August 20X1		103,200

Net assets = assets – liabilities

The trading, profit and loss account

matches revenue earned in a period with the costs incurred in earning it

Gross profit = sales – cost of sales

Net profit = gross profit – expenses

JEDSTER – TRADING, PROFIT AND LOSS
FOR THE YEAR ENDED 31 AUGUST 20X1

	£	£
Sales		80,000
Opening stock	5,000	
Purchases	40,000	
Closing stock	(10,000)	
Cost of goods sold		35,000
Gross profit		45,000
Less expenses		
Rates	12,000	
General expenses	4,000	
Wages	12,000	
Depreciation	1,000	
		29,000
Net Profit		16,000

An objective test question may ask you to explain the capital/revenue expenditure distinction

Capital expenditure results in the acquisition of fixed assets, or an increase in their earning capacity

Revenue expenditure is incurred for the purpose of trade or to maintain the existing earning capacity of the fixed assets

Notes

5: Sources, records and the books of prime entry

Topic List

The role of source documents

Sales and purchase day books

Cash books

Coding systems

This chapter covers the main sources of data and the function each source or record has.

We will see how the documents are recorded in books of prime entry to reflect business transactions.

Source documents

Business transactions are nearly always recorded on a document. These documents are the source of the information in the accounts. Such documents include the following:

- Sales order
- Purchase order
- Invoice
- Credit note
- Debit note
- Goods received note

Books of prime entry

The source documents are recorded in books of prime entry.

Journal

Journals are used to record source information that is not contained within the other books of prime entry. They record the following:

- Period end adjustments
- Correction of errors
- Large / unusual transactions

Sales day book

The sales day book is used to keep a list of all invoices sent out to customers each day. Here is an example.

SALES DAY BOOK

Date	Invoice number	Customer	Sales ledger folio	Total invoiced
				£
3.3.X9	207	ABC & Co	SL12	4,000
	208	XYZ Ltd	SL59	1,200
				5,200

Purchases day book

This is used to keep a record of invoices which a business receives. Here is an example.

PURCHASES DAY BOOK

Date	Supplier	Purchases ledger folio	Total invoiced
			£
3.4.X9	RST Ltd	PL31	215
10.4.X9	JMU plc	PL19	1,804
15.4.X9	DDT & Co	PL24	758
			2,777

There are also sales and purchase returns day books, which record goods returned by customers / to suppliers.

Cash books

Cash receipts and payments are recorded in the cash book.

Cash receipts are recorded as follows, with the total column analysed into its component parts.

CASH RECEIPTS

Date	*Narrative*	*Total* £	*Discounts allowed* £	*Sales ledger* £	*Cash sales* £	*Sundry* £
3.3.X9	Cash sale	150			150	
	Debtor: ABC & Co (discount taken)	1,000	50	1,050		
		1,150	50	1,050	150	–

Cash payments are recorded in a similar way.

CASH PAYMENTS

Date	*Narrative*	*Folio*	*Total*	*Discounts received*	*Purchases ledger*	*Cash purchases*	*Petty Cash*
			£	£	£	£	£
3.3.X9	DEF Ltd		300	–	300	–	
	Petty Cash		100	–	–	–	100
			400	–	300	–	100

Note that for accounting purposes 'cash' includes cheques, unless specified as 'cash in hand' or 'petty cash' (see next page).

Petty cash book

Most businesses keep a small amount of cash on the premises for small payments, eg stamps, coffee. Petty cash payments and receipts are recorded in a petty cash book.

PETTY CASH BOOK

RECEIPTS			PAYMENTS					
Date	*Narrative*	*Total*	*Date*	*Narrative*	*Total*	*Stationery*	*Coffee*	*etc*
		£	Date		£	£	£	£
3.3.X9	Bank	50	3.3.X9	Paper	10	10		
				Coffee	5		5	
		50			15	10	5	

Under the 'imprest system':

	£
Cash still held in petty cash	X
Plus voucher payments	X
Must equal the agreed sum or float	X

Coding systems

Each account in an accounting system has a unique code used to identify the correct account for a posting.

Advantages

- Unique identifiers
- Saves time
- Saves storage space
- Used extensively in computer systems

Example

If there are two customers called Jimmy Jewel, then a code will immediately distinguish them.

Types of code

- Sequence codes, eg 1 = saucepans, 2 = kettles
- Block codes, eg North West = 10,000 - 19,999, North East = 20,000 - 29,999
- Significant digit codes, eg 5000 = Electric light bulbs, 5060 = 60 watt bulbs
- Hierarchical codes, eg library codes: 5 = business, 52 = business/finance, 521 = Business/finance/cost accounting
- Faceted codes, eg 2/06/3/14 = Europe/England/North/Representative's name

General Ledger

The general ledger will usually use significant digit codes to signify account numbers

An objective test question in the exam could ask you to allocate a code in a given system

6: Ledger accounting and double entry

Topic List

- The nominal ledger
- Double entry bookkeeping
- The journal and imprest system
- Day book analysis
- The sales and purchase ledgers

This chapter looks at ledger accounting.

The balances on the ledgers help provide the business with information about what it is doing.

Ledger accounting

is the process by which a business keeps a record of its transactions:

- In chronological order
- Built up in cumulative totals

A ledger account or 'T' account looks like this.

NAME OF ACCOUNT

£	£
DEBIT SIDE	CREDIT SIDE

The nominal ledger

is an accounting record which summarises the financial affairs of a business. Accounts within the nominal ledger include the following.

- Plant and machinery (fixed asset)
- Stocks (current asset)
- Sales (income)
- Rent (expense)
- Total creditors (current liability)

Basic principles

Double entry bookkeeping is based on the same idea as the accounting equation.

- Every accounting transaction has two equal but opposite effects
- Equality of assets and liabilities is preserved

In a system of double entry bookkeeping every accounting event must be entered in ledger accounts both as a debit and as an equal but opposite credit.

Debit

- An increase in an expense
- An increase in an asset
- A decrease in a liability

Credit

- An increase in income
- An increase in a liability
- A decrease in an asset

Double entry bookkeeping

The rules of double entry bookkeeping are best learnt by considering the cash book.

- A *credit* entry indicates a payment made by the business; the matching debit entry is then made in an account denoting an expense paid, an asset purchased or a liability settled
- A *debit* entry in the cash book indicates cash received by the business; the matching credit entry is then made in an account denoting revenue received, a liability created or an asset realised

Journal

Format of journal entries is as follows.

Date		*(Folio)*	*Debit*	*Credit*
			£	£
DEBIT	A/c to be debited		X	
CREDIT	A/c to be credited			X

Narrative to explain transaction

Remember: the journal is used to keep a record of unusual movements between accounts

Journal entries are often required in an exam where you would not use the journal in practice. They can really test your knowledge and understanding of double entry. A multiple choice question can give you four very similar journal entries, and you have to pick the right one.

Imprest system

The double entry for topping up the petty cash is as follows:

		£	£
DEBIT	Petty cash	X	
CREDIT	Cash at bank		X

Day book analysis

Note that day books are often analysed as in the following extract (date, customer name and folio not shown).

Total invoiced	CD sales	Cassette sales
£	£	£
340	160	180
120	70	50
600	350	250
1,060	580	480

To identify sales by product, total sales would be entered ('posted') as follows.

		£	£
DEBIT	Debtors a/c	1,060	
CREDIT	Sales: CDs		580
	Sales: Cassettes		480

Other books of prime entry are analysed in a similar way.

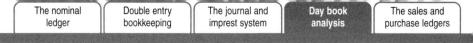

Sales and purchase ledgers

To keep track of individual customer and supplier balances it is common to maintain subsidiary ledgers called the sales ledger and the purchase ledger. Each account in these ledgers represents the balance owed by or to an individual customer or supplier.

Note that these sales and purchase ledgers are kept purely for reference and are therefore known as memorandum records. They do not form part of the double entry system.

Entries to the sales ledger are made as follows.

- When making an entry in the sales day book, an entry is then made on the debit side of the customer's account in the sales ledger
- When cash is received and an entry made in the cash book, an entry is also made on the credit side of the customer's account in the sales ledger

The purchase ledger operates in much the same way.

7: From trial balance to financial statements

Topic List

- The trial balance
- The trading, profit and loss account
- The balance sheet
- Preparing financial statements

The balances need to be extracted from the ledger accounts and entered into the trial balance.

Double entry bookkeeping dictates that the trial balance will have the same amount on the debit side as there is on the credit side.

At the end of an accounting period a balance is struck on each ledger account.

- Total all debits and credits
- Debits exceed credits = debit balance
- Credits exceed debits = credit balance

An example of balancing a ledger account is shown below.

DEBTORS

	£		£
Sales	10,000	Cash	8,000
		Balance c/d	2,000
	10,000		10,000
Balance b/d	2,000		

Trial balance

The balances are then collected in a trial balance. If the double entry is correct, total debits = total credits.

Errors

A trial balance does not guarantee accuracy. It will not pick up the following errors.

- Compensating errors
- Errors of commission
- Errors of omission
- Errors of principle

An example of a trial balance, incorporating the above debtors balance, is shown below.

ABC TRADERS TRIAL BALANCE AS AT 30 JUNE 20X7		
	£	£
Sales		35,000
Purchases	13,000	
Debtors	2,000	
Creditors		1,500
Cash	10,000	
Capital		10,000
Loan		10,000
Rent	4,000	
Sundry expenses	3,500	
Loan interest	1,000	
Drawings	5,000	
Fixtures and fittings	18,000	
	56,500	56,500

Profit and loss account

First open up a ledger account for the trading, profit and loss account. Continuing our example, this ledger account is shown below, together with the rent account to illustrate how balances are transferred to it at the end of the year.

TRADING, PROFIT AND LOSS ACCOUNT

	£		£
Purchases	13,000	Sales	35,000
Rent	4,000		
Sundry expenses	3,500		
Loan interest	1,000		

RENT

	£		£
Cash	4,000	Trading, P & L a/c	4,000
	4,000		4,000

This could be re-arranged as follows to arrive at the financial statement with which you are familiar.

ABC TRADERS
TRADING, PROFIT AND LOSS ACCOUNT
FOR THE YEAR ENDED 30 JUNE 20X7

	£	£
Sales		35,000
Cost of sales (here = purchases)		13,000
Gross profit		22,000
Expenses		
Rent	4,000	
Sundry expenses	3,500	
Loan interest	1,000	
		8,500
Net profit		13,500

Balance sheet

The balance sheet is prepared by following these steps

- Balance off the accounts relating to assets and liabilities following the debtors example shown above
- Transfer the balances on the drawings account and the trading, profit and loss account (£13,500) to the capital account as follows

You will get questions involving balance sheets and specific items in balance sheets. It is important to understand the format and how the balance sheet amounts are derived.

DRAWINGS

	£		£
Cash	5,000	Capital a/c	5,000

TRADING, PROFIT AND LOSS ACCOUNT

	£		£
Purchases	13,000	Sales	35,000
Rent	4,000		
Sundry expenses	3,500		
Loan interest	1,000		
Capital a/c	13,500		
	35,000		35,000

CAPITAL

	£		£
Drawings	5,000	Cash	10,000
Balance c/d	18,500	Trading, P & L a/c	13,500
	23,500		23,500

Prepare the balance sheet as follows

ABC TRADERS
BALANCE SHEET AS AT 30 JUNE 20X7

	£	£
Fixed assets		
Fixtures and fittings		18,000
Current assets		
Debtors	2,000	
Cash	10,000	
	12,000	
Current liabilities		
Creditors	1,500	
Loan	10,000	
	11,500	
Net current assets		500
		18,500
Proprietor's capital		18,500

Accounting process overview

This diagram summarises the topics you have revised so far. Look at it just before your exam – everything should fall into place.

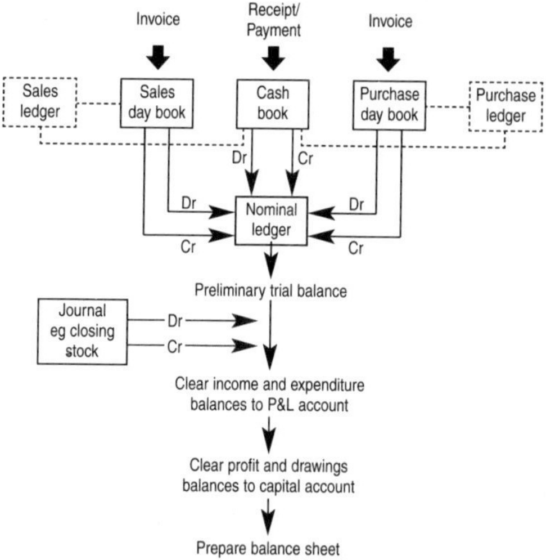

8: The cost of goods sold, accruals and prepayments

Topic List

The accounting treatment of stocks and carriage costs

Accruals and prepayments

This chapter covers the adjustments which need to be made to the cost of goods sold and expenses in order to reflect the true level of profits for the accounting period.

Formula for the cost of goods sold

	£
Opening stock value	X
Add: purchases (or production costs)	X
	X
Less: closing stock value	(X)
Cost of goods sold	X

Carriage inwards

Cost paid by purchaser of having goods transported **into** his business

Added to cost of purchases

Carriage outwards

Cost to the seller, paid by the seller, of having goods transported **out** to customer

Is a selling and distribution expense

Accrual

Expense charged against the profits of a period even though it has not yet been paid for

Prepayment

Payment made in one period but charged to the later period to which it relates

Prepayment

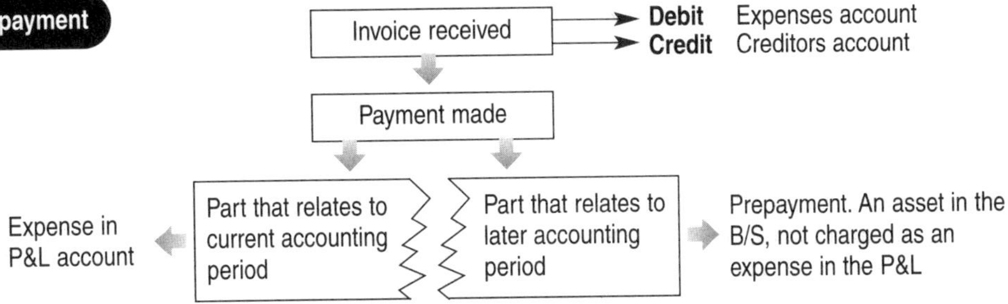

The amounted debited to the B/S will hit the P&L account in the next period.

Accruals

Expense incurred – no invoice yet

↓

Part relating to current accounting period is an accrual

Debit	P&L account
Credit	B/S creditors

Remember that the financial statements are prepared on an accruals basis and that accruals and prepayments are likely to feature in both MCQ and objective test style questions.

9: Discounts, bad debts and provisions

Topic List

Discounts

Accounting for bad and doubtful debts

This chapter looks at more adjustments. These adjustments are required before the financial statements can be prepared.

Discounts

A discount is a reduction in the price of goods or services

A supplier may have a *list* price at which he is prepared to provide his goods or services to the majority of customers. However, there may be reasons which justify a lower price or discount to particular customers or categories of customer.

It is useful to distinguish between three classes of discount

- *Trade discount* is granted to regular customers, usually those buying in bulk quantities
- *Cash discount* is granted to customers who are prepared to pay immediately in cash or by cheque, instead of purchasing on credit terms
- *Settlement discount* is granted to credit customers who pay within a specified period from the invoice date

Cash discount and settlement discount are similar in nature

- The cost of the discount to the supplier is in the nature of a financing charge, and this should be shown as an expense in the *profit and loss account*
- Discounts received by the customer are a credit in the P&L a/c

Trade discount is essentially different in nature

- It is genuinely a reduction in the selling price made in order to attract a higher level of business
- For this reason, it is accounted for as a reduction in the value of sales turnover or purchase cost shown in the *trading account*

Bad and doubtful debts

A debtor should only be classed as an asset if it is recoverable.

Bad debts

If definitely irrecoverable, the prudence concept dictates that it should be written off to the profit and loss account as a bad debt.

DEBIT Bad debt expense (P&L)
CREDIT Debtors

Doubtful debts

If uncertainty exists as to the recoverability of the debt, prudence dictates that a provision should be set up. This is offset against the debtors balance on the balance sheet.

DEBIT Doubtful debt expense
CREDIT Provision for doubtful debts

Provisions can either be specific, against a particular debtor, or general against a proportion of all debtors not specifically provided for.

When calculating the general provision to be made, the following order applies.

		£
Debtors balance per debtors control account		X
Less:	bad debts written off	(X)
	amounts specifically provided	(X)
Balance on which general provision is calculated		X

Note. Only the *movement* in the general provision needs to be accounted for.

	£
Provision required	X
Existing provision	(X)
Increase/(decrease) required	X/(X)

Subsequent recovery of debts

If a bad debt is recovered, having previously been written off, then:

DEBIT Cash
CREDIT Bad debts expense

If a doubtful debt previously provided for is recovered, then:

DEBIT Cash
CREDIT Debtors

DEBIT Provision for doubtful debts
CREDIT Doubtful debts expense

If a doubtful debt that was provided for in the prior year turns bad, then:

DEBIT Provision for doubtful debts
CREDIT Debtors

10: Accounting for stocks

Topic List

- Accounting for opening and closing stocks
- Stocktaking
- Valuing stocks
- Statutory regulations and SSAP 9 requirements

This is an important chapter, it covers a standard (SSAP 9) and the complexities surrounding the stock figure.

Remember, the stock figure affects both the balance sheet and the profit and loss account.

Entries during the year

During the year, purchases are recorded by the following entry.

DEBIT	Purchases	£ amount bought	
CREDIT	Cash or creditors		£ amount bought

The stock account is *not touched at all.*

Entries at year-end

The first thing to do is to transfer the purchases account balance to the trading account:

DEBIT	Trading	£ total purchases	
CREDIT	Purchases		£ total purchases

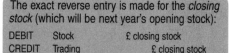

The balance on the stock account is still the *opening stock* balance. This must also be transferred to the trading account:

DEBIT	Trading	£ opening stock	
CREDIT	Stock		£ opening stock

The exact reverse entry is made for the *closing stock* (which will be next year's opening stock):

DEBIT	Stock	£ closing stock	
CREDIT	Trading		£ closing stock

Stocktaking

In order to make the entry for the closing stock, we need to know what is in stock at the year-end. We find this out *not* from the accounting records, but by going into the warehouse and actually counting the boxes on the shelves. This is a *stocktake.*

Some businesses keep detailed records of stock coming in and going out, so as not to have to count everything on the last day of the year. These records are *not* part of the double entry system.

A dealer in, say, kitchen appliances, may know from his stocktake that he has 350 toasters in stock at the year-end. He then needs to know what cash value to place on each toaster. This is the problem of valuation.

Prices

The price used to value an item of stock might be any of a number of possibilities, eg selling price, replacement cost. However, we use the lower of the following.

- The cost of buying it
- The net realisable value (NRV): the expected selling price less future costs in getting the item ready for sale and selling it

Identification rules

If we are using cost, and units have been bought at different prices during the year, we need to decide which items are left in stock at the year-end.

The possible rules are as follows. Only the first two should be used for financial accounts (as opposed to management accounts).

- FIFO: first in, first out
- Average cost
- LIFO: last in, first out
- Standard cost
- Replacement cost

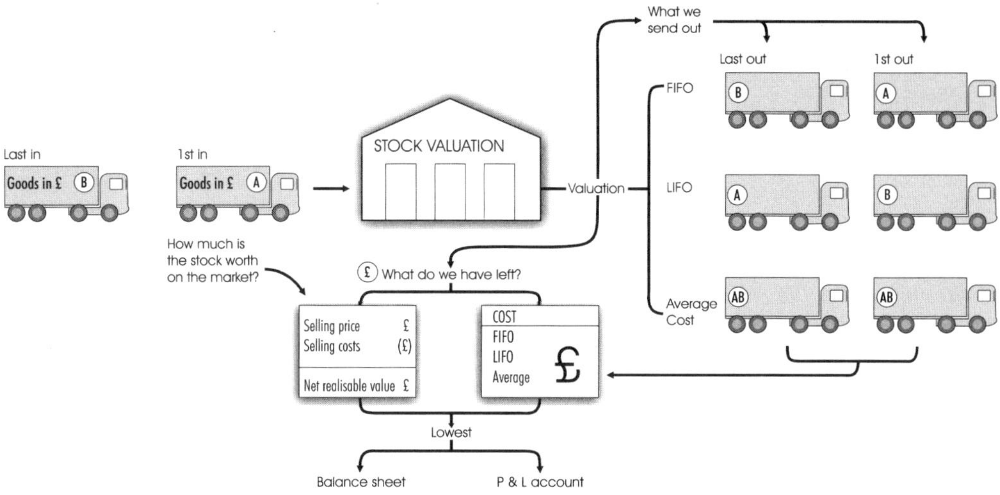
Last in
Goods in £ B
1st in
Goods in £ A
STOCK VALUATION
Valuation
What we send out
Last out
1st out
FIFO
LIFO
Average Cost
B
A
A
B
AB
AB
How much is the stock worth on the market?
£ What do we have left?
Selling price £
Selling costs (£)
Net realisable value £
COST
FIFO
LIFO
Average
£
Lowest
Balance sheet
P & L account

SSAP 9

- Stock should be valued at the lower of cost and net realisable value – the comparison between the two should ideally be made separately for each item
- Cost is the cost incurred in the normal course of business in bringing the product to its present location and condition, including production overheads and some other overheads
- Net realisable value is selling price less costs from now to completion and costs of marketing, selling and distribution
- FIFO and average cost may be used, but not LIFO

Companies Act 1985

- Stock should be grouped and disclosed as follows
  - Raw materials and consumables
  - Work in progress
  - Finished goods and goods for resale
  - Payments on account for stock not yet received
- Stock should be valued at the lower of cost and net realisable value
- Production overheads may be included in the cost of stock

11: Fixed assets – depreciation, revaluation and disposal

Topic List

Depreciation

Revaluation and disposals

Fixed assets register

Fixed assets are held in the business for a number of years use. Depreciation is the way that the fixed asset's useful life is represented in the financial statements.

You must be able to account for revaluations and disposals and to state or identify FRS 15's main provisions.

Depreciation

is a process of spreading the original cost of a fixed asset over the accounting periods in which its benefit will be felt.

- Depreciation is usually charged annually and appears as an expense in the profit and loss account
- The annual charges are also accumulated in a provision account in the balance sheet
- The credit balance on this account reflects the amount of the asset's original cost which has so far been written off

The annual depreciation charge on a fixed asset is based on two factors.

- The *depreciable amount* of the asset. This is the amount which must be written off over the entire life of the asset. It consists of the original cost less any estimated residual value
- The *estimated useful life* of the asset. This may be measured in terms of years or in terms of units of service provided by the asset

FRS 15

FRS 15 *Tangible fixed assets* makes two important points.

- Depreciation is a measure of the wearing out or depletion of a fixed asset through use, time or obsolescence
- It is a means of allocating the cost of a fixed asset over its expected useful life, so matching cost with revenues earned during that life.

Factors to consider

- Cost of the fixed asset
  - Any amount incurred that is directly attributable to bringing the asset into working condition for its intended use
  - Includes such costs as delivery costs and solicitor's fees incurred relating to the asset's acquisition
- Useful economic life (to present owner)
- Residual value

Disclosure requirements of FRS 15 over and above CA 1985:

- Depreciation methods used and the useful lives or the depreciation rates used
- Effect of revaluation of assets during the financial period (CA 1985 requires disclosure of movements on reserves including revaluation reserve)

With regard to disclosure, a proforma fixed asset note is shown here.

	Total £'000	*Land and buildings* £'000	*Plant and machinery* £'000
Cost or valuation			
At 1 January 20X7	160	100	60
Revaluation surplus	20	20	–
Additions in year	50	30	20
Disposals in year	(45)	(15)	(30)
At 31 December 20X7	185	135	50
Depreciation			
At 1 January 20X7	30	20	10
Charge for year	7	5	2
Disposals	(3)	–	(3)
At 31 December 20X7	34	25	9
Net book value			
At 31 December 20X7	151	110	41
At 1 January 20X7	130	80	50

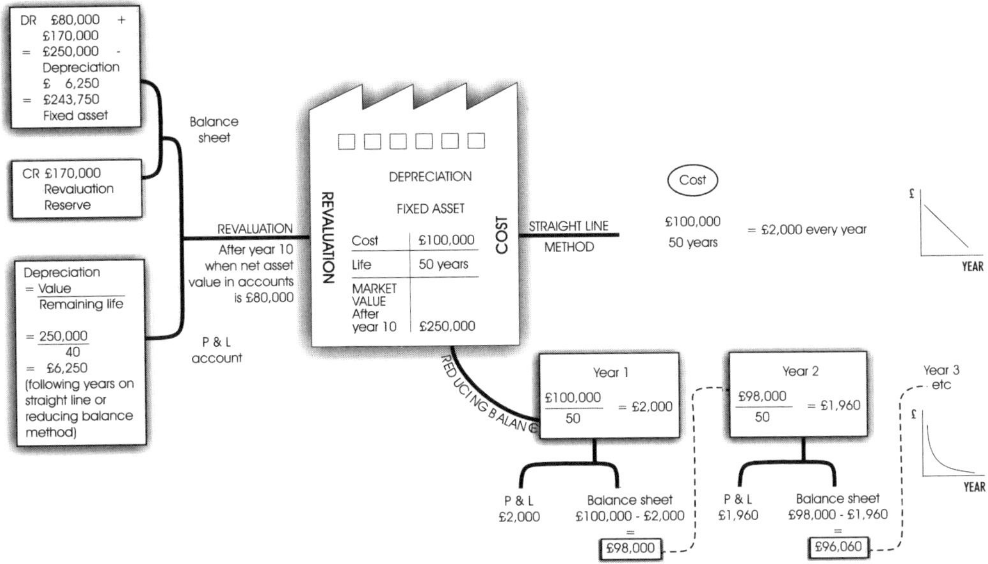
DR £80,000 + £170,000 = £250,000 - Depreciation £ 6,250 = £243,750 Fixed asset
CR £170,000 Revaluation Reserve
Depreciation = Value / Remaining life = 250,000 / 40 = £6,250 (following years on straight line or reducing balance method)
Balance sheet
P & L account
REVALUATION
After year 10 when net asset value in accounts is £80,000
REVALUATION
DEPRECIATION
FIXED ASSET
Cost £100,000
Life 50 years
MARKET VALUE After year 10 £250,000
COST
STRAIGHT LINE METHOD
Cost
£100,000 / 50 years = £2,000 every year
£
YEAR
REDUCING BALANCE
Year 1
£100,000 / 50 = £2,000
P & L £2,000
Balance sheet £100,000 - £2,000 = £98,000
Year 2
£98,000 / 50 = £1,960
P & L £1,960
Balance sheet £98,000 - £1,960 = £96,060
Year 3 etc
£
YEAR

The double entry for depreciation is as follows.

DEBIT	Depreciation expense (P&L)
CREDIT	Provision for depreciation (B/S)

This reflects:

- A periodic expense in the profit and loss account
- A decrease in the asset's value in the balance sheet

Change in expected life

If after a period of an asset's life it is realised that the original useful life has been changed, then the depreciation charge needs to be adjusted.

The revised charge from that date becomes:

$$\frac{\text{NBV at revised date}}{\text{Remaining useful life}}$$

Revaluation

This is needed in order to reflect increases in asset values and is intended to provide a fairer view of the value of the business assets.

A revaluation is recorded as follows.

DEBIT	Fixed asset (revalued amount less original cost)
DEBIT	Provision for depreciation (total depreciation to date)
CREDIT	Revaluation reserve (revalued amount less NBV)

Disposal

On disposal of an asset a profit or loss will arise depending on whether disposal proceeds are greater or less than the net book value of the asset.

- If proceeds > NBV = profit
- If proceeds < NBV = loss

You should note, however, that this profit or loss is not 'real' but simply an adjustment representing over or under depreciation during the asset's useful life.

Double entry for a disposal

- Eliminate cost

  DEBIT Disposals
  CREDIT Fixed assets

- Eliminate accumulated depreciation

  DEBIT Provision for depreciation
  CREDIT Disposals

- Account for sales proceeds

  DEBIT Cash
  CREDIT Disposals

  or if part exchange deal

  DEBIT Fixed assets
  CREDIT Disposals

  with part exchange value

- Transfer balance on disposals account to the profit and loss account

Asset Code: 938

Next depreciation: 539.36

A	Description:	1 * Seisha Laser printer YCA40809
B	Date of purchase:	25/05/X6
C	Cost:	1618.25
D	Accumulated depreciation:	584.35
E	Depreciation %:	33.33%
F	Depreciation type:	straight line
G	Date of disposal:	NOT SET
H	Sale proceeds:	0.00
I	Accumulated depreciation amount:	55Q O/EQPT DEP CHARGE
J	Depreciation expense account:	34F DEPN O/EQPT
K	Depreciation period:	standard
L	Comments:	electronic office
M	Residual value:	0.00
N	Cost account:	65C O/E ADDITIONS

12: Bank reconciliations

Topic List

Bank statement and cash book

The bank reconciliation

This topic features regularly in the exam. You will probably be given the cash book balance and a number of adjustments and asked to calculate the bank statement balance - or vice versa.

Bank reconciliation

A comparison of a bank statement with the cash book.

The bank reconciliation is an important financial control. The bank reconciliation will invariably show a difference.

Differences on bank reconciliation

Errors: more likely on the cash book.

Omissions: items on the bank statement not in the cash book (e.g. bank charges)

Timing differences: cheques issued and entered in the cash book but not yet presented at the bank for instance.

Proforma bank reconciliation

CASH ACCOUNT

	£		£
Balance b/f	X	Dishonoured cheque	X
		Bank charges	X
		Standing orders	X
Undercast error		Direct debits	X
in balance b/f	X	Balance c/f	X
	X		X
Adjusted balance b/f	X		

	£
Balance per bank statement	X
Less outstanding cheques	(X)
Plus outstanding lodgements	X
Plus/less bank errors	X/(X)
Balance per adjusted cash account	X

Notes

13: Control accounts

Topic List

What are control accounts?

The operation of control accounts

The purpose of control accounts

Control accounts help highlight human error. They also allow last minute adjustments for items such as bad debts.

You may have to calculate the balance on a control account or a reconciled cash book as part of an objective test question or multiple choice question.

What are control accounts?

A control account is a *total* account.

- Its balance represents an asset or a liability which is the grand total of many individual assets or liabilities
- These individual assets/liabilities must be separately detailed in subsidiary accounting records, but their total is conveniently available in the control account ready for immediate use

Most businesses operate control accounts for trade debtors and creditors, but such accounts may be useful in other areas too, eg VAT.

With regard to the double entry relating to debtors and creditors, note the following.

- The accounts of individuals are maintained *for memorandum purposes only*
- Entering a sales invoice, say, in the account of an individual debtor is not part of the double entry process

The diagram on the next page illustrates how sales invoices are introduced into the double entry system.

The invoices in the sales day book are totalled periodically and the total amount is posted as follows.

DEBIT	Debtors control account
CREDIT	Sales account

Similarly, the total of cash receipts from debtors is posted from the cash book to the credit of the debtors control account.

In the same way, the creditors control account is credited with the total purchase invoices logged in the purchase day book and debited with the total of cash payments to suppliers.

Overview of invoice processing

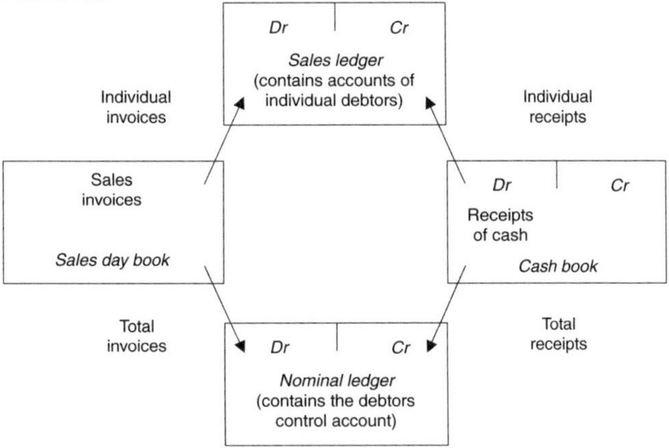

Reasons for maintaining control accounts

It is worth bearing in mind the main reasons for maintaining both individual accounts and a control account.

- The individual accounts are necessary for administrative convenience. For example, a customer may wish to query the balance he owes to the business; to deal with his query, sales ledger staff would refer to his individual account
- The control accounts provide a convenient total which can be used immediately in extracting a trial balance or preparing accounts.
- A reconciliation between the control account total and the sales ledger will help to detect errors, thus providing an important control

Proforma control account reconciliation

SALES LEDGER CONTROL ACCOUNT

	£		£
Unadjusted balance b/f	X	Contra with purchase ledger control a/c	X
Sales daybook Undercast	X	Discounts allowed not recorded	X
Dishonoured cheques	X	Transposition error	X
		Adjusted bal c/f	X
	X		X
Balance b/f	X		

TOTAL OF BALANCES EXTRACTED FROM SALES LEDGER

		£
Original total		X
Add:	Debit balance on X Ltd's account extracted as credit balance (= credit balance × 2)	X
	Miscast of Y Ltd's account	X
	Z Ltd's balance omitted	X
Less:	Contra with purchase ledger	(X)
	Bad debt written off	(X)
	Discounts allowed not recorded	(X)
Total as per amended control account		X

Note. Follow the same approach for purchase ledger control account reconciliations.

It is the adjusted balance that appears in the final set of accounts.

Possible reasons for credit balances on debtors (ie sales ledger) accounts, or for debit balances on creditors (ie purchase ledger) accounts

- Overpayment of amount owed
- Return of goods
- Payment in advance
- Posting errors

14: Accounting for value added tax

Topic List

The nature of VAT and how it is collected

Accounting for VAT

VAT is a general consumer expenditure tax. There is likely to be an MCQ on it.

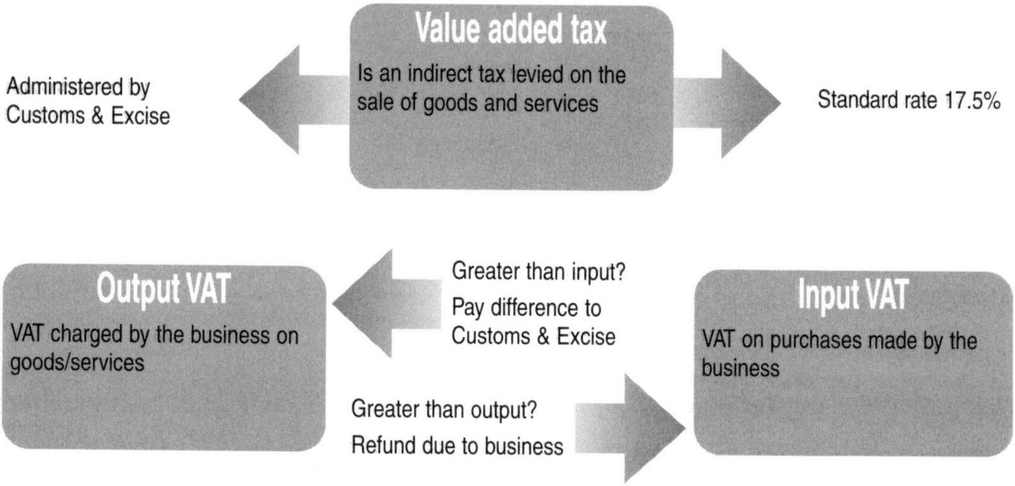
Value added tax
Is an indirect tax levied on the sale of goods and services
Administered by Customs & Excise
Standard rate 17.5%
Output VAT
VAT charged by the business on goods/services
Greater than input?
Pay difference to Customs & Excise
Input VAT
VAT on purchases made by the business
Greater than output?
Refund due to business

a Credit sales

(i) Include VAT in sales day book; show it separately

(ii) Include gross receipts from debtors in cashbook; no need to show VAT separately

(iii) Exclude VAT element from profit and loss account

(iv) Credit VAT creditor with output VAT element of sales invoices

b Credit purchases

(i) Include VAT in purchases day book; show it separately

(ii) Include gross payments in cashbook; no need to show VAT separately

(iii) Exclude recoverable VAT from profit and loss account

(iv) Include irrecoverable VAT in profit and loss account

(v) Debit VAT creditor with recoverable input VAT element of credit purchases

c Cash sales

(i) Include gross receipts in cashbook; show VAT separately

(ii) Exclude VAT element from profit and loss account

(iii) Credit VAT creditor with output VAT element of cash sales

d Cash purchases

(i) Include gross payments in cashbook: show VAT separately

(ii) Exclude recoverable VAT from profit and loss account

(iii) Include irrecoverable VAT in profit and loss account

(iv) Debit VAT creditor with recoverable input VAT element of cash purchases

15: Accounting for wages and salaries

Topic List

- Gross pay and deductions
- Accounting for wages and salaries

There will probably be an MCQ on this topic.

Definitions

Gross pay is the full amount that an employee earns

Deductions are the amounts taken from gross pay for income tax, NIC and any other reasons agreed by the employer and employee, eg pension contributions.

Net pay is gross pay less deductions, ie the amount actually received by the employee

Wages and salaries are usually accounted for involving a wages control account.

Once all the entries have been posted, the balance on the control account should be zero.

A detailed example follows. Make sure you can understand the entries made.

At 1 June 20X7 Netpay Ltd had the following credit balances on ledger accounts.

	£
PAYE control account	4,750
NIC control account	4,590
Employee savings account	1,373

The company's wages records for the month of June 20X7 showed the following.

	£
Total gross pay	27,294
PAYE	6,101
Employer's NIC	2,612
Employees' NIC	2,240
Employees' savings deductions	875
Net amounts paid to employees	18,078

The company paid £9,340 to Inland Revenue during the month, being £4,750 PAYE and £4,590 NIC.

You are required to show the ledger accounts recording these transactions.

Solution

WAGES CONTROL ACCOUNT

	£		£
PAYE control	6,101	Wages expense a/c:	
NIC control:		gross pay	27,294
employees' contributions	2,240		
Employee savings a/c	875		
Bank: net pay	18,078		
	27,294		27,294

PAYE CONTROL ACCOUNT

	£		£
Bank	4,750	Balance b/f	4,750
Balance c/d	6,101	Wages control	6,101
	10,851		10,851
		Balance b/d	6,101

NIC CONTROL ACCOUNT

	£		£
Bank	4,590	Balance b/f	4,590
Balance c/d	4,852	Wages control:	
		employees' NIC	2,240
		Wages expense a/c:	
		employer's NIC	2,612
	9,442		9,442
		Balance b/d	4,852

EMPLOYEE SAVINGS ACCOUNT

	£		£
Balance c/d	2,248	Balance b/f	1,373
		Wages control	875
	2,248		2,248
		Balance b/d	2,248

Note. This account shows the company's liability to employees, who may wish to withdraw their savings at any time.

In the past, this topic has caused unnecessary problems. As long as you understand the principles of control accounts and follow through the double entry logically, you should not experience too many difficulties. Do not be put off by the 'tax' content. PAYE is just another creditor.

16: Correction of errors. Preparation of final accounts

Topic List

- Types of error in accounting
- The correction of errors
- Preparation of final accounts

There will always be errors which need to be corrected before the final accounts can be prepared.

It helps to know what kind of errors can be made in order that you can find them and then correct them.

Types of error

The main types of error are as follows

- Errors of transposition, e.g. writing £381 as £318 (the difference in such errors is always divisible by 9)
- Errors of omission, eg receive supplier's invoice for £500 and do not record it in the books at all
- Errors of principle, eg treating capital expenditure as revenue expenditure
- Errors of commission, eg putting telephone expenses of £250 in the electricity expense account
- Compensating errors, eg both sales day book and purchases day book coincidentally undercast by £500

Correction of errors

Errors can be corrected using the journal, but only those errors which required both a debit and an (equal) credit adjustment. Consider the following examples

Example

Accountant omits to record invoice from supplier for £2,000. This would be corrected by the following journal entry.

DEBIT	Purchases	£2,000	
CREDIT	Creditors		£2,000

A transaction previously omitted.

Example

Accountant posts car insurance of £800 to motor vehicles account. Correct as follows.

DEBIT	Motor expenses	£800	
CREDIT	Motor vehicles		£800

Correction of error of principle.

A suspense account is a temporary account that is used in the following circumstances.

- The bookkeeper knows in which account to make the debit entry for a transaction but does not know where to make the corresponding credit entry (or vice versa)
- The credit is temporarily posted to the suspense account until the correct credit entry is known
- A difference occurs in the trial balance caused by the incomplete recording of the double entry in respect of one or more transactions
- The difference is recorded in the suspense account and included in the trial balance, so restoring equality

Any balance on a suspense account must be eliminated. It is *never* included in the final accounts.

Example

Harry Perkins, sole trader, prepared his trial balance for the year ended 30 June 20X5. To his dismay he found that debits exceeded credits by £7,452.

He has discovered the following errors.

- Discounts allowed of £486 were posted to the discounts allowed account as £684
- Credit sales totalling £7,500 had not been posted to the sales account
- The balance on the accruals account of £404 had been omitted when the trial balance was prepared
- In respect of telephone expenses of £650, the only entry to have been made was in the cash account.

The balance would be cleared by writing up the suspense account as follows.

SUSPENSE ACCOUNT

	£		£
Discounts allowed (1)	198	B/d	7,452
Sales (2)	7,500	Telephone (4)	650
Accruals (3)	404		
	8,102		8,102

			£	£
(1)	The correct entry :			
	DEBIT	Discounts allowed	486	
	CREDIT	Debtors		486
	The actual entry:			
	DEBIT	Discount allowed	684	
	CREDIT	Debtors		486
	∴ CREDIT	Suspense (balance)		198
	To correct:			
	DEBIT	Suspense	198	
	CREDIT	Discounts allowed		198

			£	£
(2)	The correct entry :			
	DEBIT	Debtors	7,500	
	CREDIT	Sales		7,500
	The actual entry:			
	DEBIT	Debtors	7,500	
	∴ CREDIT	Suspense		7,500
	To correct:			
	DEBIT	Suspense	7,500	
	CREDIT	Sales		7,500
(3)	To correct:			
	DEBIT	Suspense	404	
	CREDIT	Accruals		404
(4)	To correct:			
	DEBIT	Telephone	650	
	CREDIT	Suspense		650

With suspense accounts it is essential to think carefully about double entry. Provided you are calm there is no reason why you should not get it right.

Final accounts

You have now revised all areas necessary to prepare the final accounts of a sole trader. Areas you should be totally familiar with are as follows.

- Ledger accounts
- Trial balance
- Format of profit and loss account and balance sheet
- Adjustments
  - Depreciation
  - Stock
  - Accruals and prepayments
  - Bad and doubtful debts

17: The accounts of unincorporated organisations

Topic List

Receipts and payments account

Income and expenditure account

Preparing income and expenditure accounts

This chapter deals with non-trading organisations, such as clubs, societies and charities.

Such organisations do not produce a profit and loss account, but a receipts and payments account (for small clubs) or an income and expenditure account.

Receipts and payments account

Many small unincorporated organisations have little need for full accounts. They just keep a receipts and payments account which is a summary of the organisation's cash book.

No balance sheet is produced with a receipts and payments account.

PROFORMA RECEIPTS AND PAYMENTS A/C

	£		£
Receipts		*Payments*	
Balance b/f	X	Bar expenses	X
Bar takings	X	Rent	X
Subscriptions	X	Wages	X
		Stationery	X
		Van*	X
		Balance c/f	X
	X		X

* Note. Capital expenditure also included.

Advantages

- Easy; quite sufficient for small clubs with simple transactions
- Forms basis for income and expenditure account and balance sheet

Disadvantages

- Does not deal with money owing or prepaid
- Does not take account of depreciation
- Does not distinguish capital and revenue expenditure

Income and expenditure account

This is very similar to a profit and loss account for a trading organisation. However non-trading organisations do not make profits. Therefore the difference between income and expenditure is called a **surplus** or **deficit**, rather than a profit or loss. The capital of the organisation is called the **accumulated fund**.

Sources of income

- Membership subscriptions
- Payments for life membership
- 'Profits' from bar sales
- 'Profits' from sales of food in the club cafe
- 'Profits' from social events, eg dances
- Interest received on investments

Special funds

- Funds received for special purposes must be kept separate from general funds
- Interest received is credited to the special purpose fund

PROFORMA INCOME AND EXPENDITURE A/C

	£	£
Income		
Subscriptions		X
Life memberships		X
*Trading activity profit		X
Bank interest received		X
*Surplus on club event		X
*Profit on sale of fixed asset		X
		X
Expenditure		
Rent	X	
Rates	X	
Electricity	X	
Depreciation	X	
*Loss on trading activity	X	
*Loss on club event	X	
*Loss on sale of fixed asset	X	
	(X)	
Surplus/(deficit) of income over expenditure	X/(X)	

* Alternatives

PROFORMA BALANCE SHEET

		Accumulated	*Net*
book			
	Cost	*depreciation*	*value*
	£	£	£
Fixed assets			
Fixtures and fittings	X	X	X
Investments			X
			X
Current assets			
Stock		X	
Trade debtors		X	
Subscriptions in arrears		X	
Prepayments		X	
Cash at bank		X	
		X	
Current liabilities			
Trade creditors		X	
Subscriptions in advance		X	
Accruals		X	
Memberships		X	
		X	
Net current assets			X
			X
Accumulated fund			
Opening balance			X
Profit/(loss) on sale of investments			X/(X)
Surplus/(deficit) of income over expenditure for the period			X/(X)
			X

Income and expenditure account

Examination questions are likely to give you the following information.

- Receipts and payments account
- Balance of assets and liabilities at beginning of period
- Details of period end accruals and prepayments

Typically you will need to carry out the following tasks.

- Calculate the balance on the accumulated fund at the beginning of the period
- Calculate the balance on the cash book
- Calculate the amount of cash stolen from the business
- Calculate a key figure such as sales or purchases

Subscriptions

Subscriptions will be the main source of income. They are normally paid for in advance.

It is important to ensure that subscriptions received and receivable are recorded in the correct period.

Example

Consider the subscription accounts of a club as at 31 December 20X7.

Members paid £1 pa in 20X6 and £2 pa in 20X7 and 20X8.

At 31.12.X6	5 members had not yet paid last year's subs	2 had paid in advance
At 31.12.X7	4 members had not paid their 20X7 subs	10 had paid in advance for 20X8

Cash received in respect of subscriptions in 20X7 was £63.

The subscription income for the year would be calculated as follows.

SUBSCRIPTIONS

	£		£
Opening debtors (1.1.X7)	5	Opening income in advance (1.1.X7)	4
Income and expenditure account (20X7 sub income)	50	Cash	63
Closing subs in advance (creditors c/d: 31.12.X7)	20	Closing arrears (debtors c/d: 31.12.X7)	8
	75		75

Life membership subscriptions

This is a one-off payment, usually paid at the time a person becomes a life member.

On receipt of the money, the accounting entry is:

DEBIT Cash
CREDIT Life membership fund (in balance sheet)

There are two methods of taking the life membership subscription to the income and expenditure account.

1. Keep the money in the life membership fund until the member dies, and then transfer whole amount to the income and expenditure account.

   DEBIT Life membership fund
   CREDIT Income and expenditure account

2 Release the receipt to the income and expenditure account over the life of the member.

In practice, an average life-time is chosen, eg 20 years is taken to be the average time that a person remains a member.

Annual transfer is therefore one twentieth of balance on life membership fund.

DEBIT Life membership fund
CREDIT Income and expenditure account

The second method is preferable.

- It avoids the need to record the death of individual members
- It applies the matching concept: the revenue from a life membership subscription is more correctly income relating to the whole of a member's life-time, rather than income arising on a member's death

Bar profits

Bar/restaurant profits represent a trading activity. The net profit or loss on these activities is shown in the income and expenditure account. A separate statement indicating how the net profit or loss was arrived at is often required.

Social events

Social events such as the Christmas dinner involve both receipts and payments. The net of these is shown in the income and expenditure account.

Sale of fixed assets

If the asset was being depreciated, take the resultant profit/loss to income and expenditure account. If not depreciated, take the profit/loss to the accumulated fund.

Investments

Clubs may make investments.

- Investment income is recorded in the income and expenditure account
- Profit/loss on the sale of an investment is taken to the accumulated fund and it is not a normal trading activity

18: Incomplete records

Topic List

- Opening balance sheet
- Credit sales, purchases and cost of sales
- Stolen or destroyed goods
- Cash book
- Accruals, prepayments and drawings

This area is a very good test of your accounts preparation knowledge.

You need to know how the accounts fit together in order to fill the blanks.

Types of question

An incomplete records question may require competence in dealing with one or more of the following.

- Theft of cash (balance on the cash in hand account is unknown)
- Theft or destruction of stock (closing stock is the unknown)
- Estimated figures, eg 'drawings are between £15 and £20 per week'
- Calculation of capital by means of net assets
- Calculation of profit by P = increase in net assets plus drawings minus increase in capital (business equation)
- Calculation of year end stock when the stocktake was done after the year end

These are all figures which you may be asked to calculate

Opening balance sheet

Often an examination question provides information about the assets and liabilities of a business at the beginning of a period, leaving you to calculate capital as the balancing figure.

Remember

Assets - liabilities = Proprietor's capital

Credit sales and debtors

The key lies in the formula linking sales, cash receipts and debtors.

Remember

Opening debtors + sales - cash receipts = closing debtors

Alternatively put all the workings into a control account to calculate the figure you want.

Purchases and trade creditors

Similarly you need a formula for linking purchases, cash payments and creditors.

Opening creditors + purchases - cash payments = closing creditors

Use a control account.

DEBTORS CONTROL ACCOUNT

	£		£
Opening debtors	X	Cash receipts	X
Sales	X	Closing debtors	X
	X		X

CREDITORS CONTROL ACCOUNT

	£		£
Cash payments	X	Opening creditors	X
Closing creditors	X	Purchases	X
	X		X

Gross margins and mark ups

Other incomplete records problems revolve around the relationship between sales, cost of sales and gross profit: in other words, they are based on reconstructing a trading account. Bear in mind the crucial formula:

		%
	Cost of sales	100
Plus	Gross profit	25
Equals	Sales	125

Gross profit may be expressed either as a percentage of cost of sales or as a percentage of sales.

- In the example, gross profit is 25% of cost of sales (ie 25/100). The terminology is a 25% *mark up*
- Gross profit can also be expressed as 20% of sales (ie 25/125). The terminology is a 20% gross *margin* or *gross profit percentage*. The proforma would appear as follows.

		%
	Cost of sales	80
Plus	Gross profit	20
Equals	Sales	100

Stolen goods or goods destroyed

The cost of goods stolen/destroyed can be calculated as follows.

	£
Cost of goods sold based on gross profit margin or mark up	A
Cost of goods sold calculated using standard formula (ie opening stock plus purchases less closing stock)	(B)
Difference (lost/stolen stock)	C

- If no goods have been lost, A and B should be the same and therefore C should be nil
- If goods have been lost, B will be larger than A, because some goods which have been purchased were neither sold nor remaining in stock, ie they have been lost
- Stolen or lost stock is accounted for in two ways depending on whether the goods were insured

If insured

DEBIT	Insurance claim (debtor)
CREDIT	Trading account

If not insured

DEBIT	Profit and loss account
CREDIT	Trading account

Cash book

Incomplete records problems often concern small retail businesses where sales are mainly for cash. A two-column cash book is often the key to preparing final accounts.

- The bank column records cheques drawn on the business bank account and cheques received from customers and other sources
- The cash column records till receipts and any expenses or drawings paid out of till receipts before banking

Debits (receipts)		Credits (payments)	
Cash £	Bank £	Cash £	Bank £

Don't forget that movements between cash and bank need to be recorded by contra entries. This will usually be cash receipts lodged in the bank (debit bank column, credit cash column), but could also be withdrawals of cash from the bank to top up the till (debit cash column, credit bank column).

Again, incomplete records problems will often feature an unknown figure to be derived. Enter in the credit of the cash column all amounts known to have been paid from till receipts: expenses, drawings, lodgements into bank. Enter in the debit of the cash column all receipts from cash customers or other cash sources.

- The balancing figure may then be a large debit, representing the value of cash sales if that is the unknown figure
- Alternatively it may be a credit entry that is needed to balance, representing the amount of cash drawings or of cash stolen

Accruals and prepayments

When there is an accrued expense or prepayment, the P & L charge can be calculated from the opening balance, the cash movement and the closing balance.

Sometimes it helps to use a 'T' account, eg as follows (for a rent payment).

RENT

	£		£
Prepayment: bal b/f	700	P & L a/c (bal fig)	9,000
Cash	9,300	Prepayment: bal c/f	1,000
	10,000		10,000

Drawings

Note three tricky points about drawings.

- Owner pays personal income into business bank account

  DEBIT Cash
  CREDIT Capital (or drawings)

- Owner pays personal expenses out of business bank account

  DEBIT Drawings
  CREDIT Cash

- Wording of an exam question
  - 'Drawings approximately £40 per week'
    ∴ Drawings for year = £40 × 52 = £2,080
  - 'Drawings between £35 and £45 per week'
    ∴ Drawings are a missing number to be calculated

Step by step approach

Find opening balances – may need to find opening capital using the accounting equation

Net assets = proprietor's interest

Set out the following (as far as possible)

- Trading, profit and loss account
- Balance sheet

Open 'T' accounts

- Cash account or two column cash book
- Bank account or two column cash book
- Debtors control account
- Creditors control account

As the exam will be in CBA format, incomplete records will probably feature in short questions, asking you to find one figure eg value of stock destroyed. But you may have some longer workings to do, so use a step-by-step approach and deal with each item methodically.

19: Limited companies

Topic List

- Limited companies
- Shares and dividends
- Taxation
- Balance sheet and P&L

This section looks at limited company accounts for external purposes.

Limited company accounts are more comprehensive as there are more stakeholders who wish to know how the business is doing.

Features

Limited companies offer limited liability to their owners (shareholders). If the company becomes insolvent, the maximum amount that an owner stands to lose is his share of the capital of the business. This is an attractive prospect to investors. Limited companies may be private (ltd) or public (plc).

The main features of limited companies are as follows:

- Owners = shareholders or members
- Large number of owners
- Owner/manager split
- Owners appoint directors to run business on their behalf
- Owners receive share of profits in form of dividends

- Regulation under CA 1985
  - Annual published accounts
  - Accounting records
  - Statutory registers
  - Audit

Funding

Companies are funded in the following ways:

- Retained profits
- Short term liabilities (creditors etc)
- Share capital
- Debenture loans

Shares

The proprietors' capital in a limited company consists of share capital. When a company is set up for the first time it issues shares, which are paid for by investors, who then become shareholders of the company.

Shares are denominated in units of 25 pence, 50 pence, £1 or whatever seems appropriate. This is referred to as their nominal value.

Preference shares are characterised as follows

- Rights depend on articles
- Right to fixed dividend with priority over ordinary shares
- Do not usually carry voting rights
- Generally priority for capital in winding up
- May be cumulative or non-cumulative

Ordinary shares have the following characteristics

- No right to fixed dividend
- Entitled to remaining profits after preference dividend
- Entitled to surplus on repayment of capital

Share capital

- *Authorised.* The maximum amount of share capital that a company is empowered to issue
- *Issued.* The amount of share capital that has been issued to shareholders. The amount of issued capital cannot exceed the amount of authorised capital
- *Called up.* When shares are issued or allotted, a company does not always expect to be paid the full amount of the issue price at once. It might instead call up only a part of the issue price, and call up the remainder later
- *Paid-up.* Called up capital that has been paid.
- *Market value.* This is the price at which someone is prepared to purchase the share value from an existing shareholder. It is different from nominal value

Debentures

Companies may issue debentures or loan stock. These are long term liabilities not capital. They differ from shares as follows:

- Shareholder = owner; debentureholder = creditor
- Debenture interest *must* be paid; not so dividends
- Debentures often secured on company assets

Reserves

Revenue reserves consist of distributable profits and can be paid out as dividends

- Profit and loss reserve
- Others, as the directors decide, eg general reserve

Capital reserves are not available for distribution. They include the following:

- *Share premium.* Section 130 of the Companies Act 1985 requires that whenever shares are issued for a consideration in excess of their nominal value such a premium shall be credited to a share premium account
- Share premium account can be used to
  - Issue bonus shares
  - Write off formation expenses and premium on the redemption of shares and debentures
  - Write off the expenses on a new issue of shares/debentures and the discount on the issue of debentures
- *Revaluation reserve.* Created when a company revalues one or more of its fixed assets

Dividends

Dividends are appropriations of profit after tax. They may be paid in two stages, interim and final, and may be expressed as a percentage (of nominal value) or as pence per share.

Dividends proposed at the end of the year will not yet have been paid, so they will appear as a current liability in the balance sheet.

DEBIT P&L appropriation

CREDIT Dividend payable (creditor)

Tax

Companies pay corporation tax on their profits. Part of the tax is paid during the course of the year. The balance of the charge for the year will be a taxation creditor included under current liabilities in the balance sheet.

DEBIT P&L account
CREDIT Taxation payable (creditor)

TYPICAL COMPANY LIMITED
BALANCE SHEET AS AT ....

	£	£	£
Fixed assets			
Intangible assets			
Development costs		X	
Concessions, patents, licences, trademarks		X	
Goodwill		X	
			X
Tangible assets			
Land and buildings		X	
Plant and machinery		X	
Fixtures, fittings, tools and equipment		X	
Motor vehicles		X	
			X
Investments			X
			X
Current assets			
Stocks		X	
Debtors and prepayments		X	
Investments		X	
Cash at bank and in hand		X	
		X	
Creditors: amounts falling due within one year (ie current liabilities)			
Debenture loans (nearing their redemption date)	X		
Bank overdraft and loans	X		
Trade creditors	X		
Bills of exchange payable	X		
Taxation	X		
Accruals	X		
Proposed dividends	X		
		(X)	

	£	£	£
Net current assets			X
Total assets less current liabilities			X
Creditors: amounts falling due after more than one year			
Debenture loans	X		
Taxation	X		
			(X)
			X
Capital and reserves			
Called up share capital			
Ordinary shares		X	
Preference shares		X	
			X
Reserves			
Share premium account		X	
Revaluation reserve		X	
Other reserves		X	
Profit and loss account (retained profits)		X	
			X
			X

TYPICAL COMPANY LIMITED
PROFIT AND LOSS ACCOUNT
FOR THE YEAR ENDED ...

	£	£
Turnover		X
Cost of sales		(X)
Gross profit		X
Distribution costs	X	
Administrative expenses	X	
		(X)
Operating profit		X
Income from fixed investments	X	
Other interest receivable and similar income	X	
		X
Interest payable		(X)
Profit before tax		X
Tax		(X)
Profit after tax		X
Appropriations:		
Dividends: preference	X	
ordinary	X	
Transfer to general reserve	X	
		(X)
Retained profit for the year		X
P&L a/c as at the beginning of the year		X
P&L a/c as at the end of the year		X

20: Manufacturing accounts and cash flow statements

Topic List

- Manufacturing accounts
- FRS 1 Cash flow statements
- Preparing a cash flow

Manufacturing accounts provide extra information about the cost of manufacturing goods for sale.

Profit is not the same as cash. The cash flow statement allows us to assess the quality of profit. How quickly does the profit figure get translated into a healthy cash balance?

It is possible for a profitable firm to collapse due to poor cash flows.

For a manufacturing company, there are two main aspects to performance.

- Production operations (manufacturing account)
- Trading activities (trading account)

A manufacturing account aims to show the cost of producing finished goods stock. The elements included in manufacturing cost are arranged in a logical order.

- The account begins with the cost of raw materials consumed in the period: opening stock plus purchases (including carriage inwards) less closing stock
- The cost of direct labour is then added to arrive at the prime cost of production
- The next step is the calculation of factory overheads
- Finally, there is an adjustment in respect of work in progress (WIP)
  - Opening WIP has been used up during the year and is therefore added to the cost of producing finished goods
  - The cost of closing WIP is a deduction from the factory cost of finished goods
- The factory cost of finished goods produced may then be transferred to the trading account as part of the cost of goods sold

You may be asked to calculate prime cost or factory cost of finished goods.

MANUFACTURING ACCOUNT
FOR THE YEAR ENDED 31 DECEMBER 20X6

	£	£
Raw materials		
Opening stock	4,000	
Purchases (net of returns)	207,000	
	211,000	
Less closing stock	23,000	
		188,000
Factory wages		21,000
Prime cost		209,000
Production overhead		
Factory power	4,000	
Plant depreciation	3,000	
Plant maintenance	1,500	
Rates and insurance	2,500	
Light and heat	3,000	
Sundry expenses	5,000	
Factory manager's salary	9,000	
Building depreciation	1,000	
		29,000
Production cost of resources consumed		238,000
Work in progress		
Opening stocks	8,000	
Closing stocks	(17,000)	
Increase in work in progress stocks		(9,000)
Production cost of finished goods produced		229,000

The trading, profit and loss account for the same firm might appear as follows.

	£	£
Sales		340,000
Opening stock of finished goods	40,000	
Cost of finished goods produced	229,000	
	269,000	
Closing stock of finished goods	(30,000)	
Cost of goods sold		239,000
Gross profit		101,000
Expenses		70,000
Net profit		31,000

Purpose

A cash flow statement shows the effect of a company's commercial transactions on its cash balance.

It is thought that users of accounts can readily understand cash flows, as opposed to profit and loss accounts and balance sheets, which are subject to manipulation by the use of different accounting policies.

Cash flows are used in investment appraisal methods such as net present value and hence a cash flow statement gives potential investors the chance to evaluate a business.

Format

FRS 1 (revised) *Cash flow statements* splits cash flows into the following headings:

- Net cash flow from operating activities
- Taxation
- Equity dividends paid
- Return on investments and servicing of finance - covering investment income, interest paid and dividends paid
- Capital expenditure - acquisition and disposal of fixed assets and of current assets not included in liquid resources
- Management of liquid resources - eg purchase and sale of treasury stock
- Financing - covering the issue and redemption of long-term debt and shares

The FRS requires two reconciliations

- Operating profit and the net cash flow from operating activities
- The movement of cash in the period and the movement of net debt

Neither reconciliation forms part of the cash flow statement but each may be given either adjoining the statement or in a separate note.

PROFORMA CASH FLOW STATEMENT FOR THE YEAR ENDED 31 DECEMBER 20X0

Reconciliation of operating profit to net cash inflow from operating activities

	£'000
Operating profit	X
Depreciation charges	X
Increase in stocks	(X)
Increase in debtors	(X)
Increase in creditors	X
Net cash inflow from operating activities	X

CASH FLOW STATEMENT

Net cash inflow from operating activities	X
Returns on investments and servicing of finance (note 1)	X
Taxation	(X)
Capital expenditure (note 1)	(X)
	X
Equity dividends paid	(X)
	X
Management of liquid resources (note 1)	(X)
Financing (note 1)	X
Increase in cash	X

Reconciliation of net cash flow to movement in net debt (Note 2)

	£'000	£'000
Increase in cash in period	X	
Cash to repurchase debenture	X	
Cash used to increase liquid resources	X	
Change in net debt*		X
Net debt at 1.1.X0		(X)
Net funds at 31.12.X0		X

*In this example all changes in net debt are cash flows.

NOTES TO THE CASH FLOW STATEMENT

		£'000	£'000
1	*Gross cash flows*	£'000	
	Returns on investment and servicing of finance		
	Interest received	X	
	Interest paid	(X)	
			X
	Capital expenditure		
	Payments to acquire intangible fixed assets	(X)	
	Payments to acquire tangible fixed assets	(X)	
	Receipts from sale of tangible fixed assets	X	
			(X)
	Management of liquid resources		
	Purchase of treasury bills	(X)	
	Sale of treasury bills	X	
			(X)
	Financing		
	Issue of ordinary share capital	X	
	Repurchase of debenture loan	(X)	
	Expenses paid in connection with share issues	(X)	
			X

2 *Analysis of changes in net debt*

	At 1 Jan 20X0	Cash flows	Other changes	At 31 Dec 20X0
	£'000	£'000	£'000	£'000
Cash in hand, at bank	X	X		X
Overdrafts	(X)	X		
		X		
Debt due within 1 year	(X)	X	(X)	(X)
Debt due after 1 year	(X)		X	(X)
Current asset investments	X	X		X
Total	(X)	X	X	X

The figures in boxes should agree to the appropriate parts of the cash flow statement.

The above proforma was for the *indirect method.* The *direct method* proforma is the same except for the first part which appears as follows.

	£	£
Cash received from customers	X	
Cash paid to suppliers	(X)	
Cash paid to and on behalf of employees	(X)	
Net cash inflow from operating activities		X

Examination questions will probably require you to apply the indirect method. If the direct method is required, the necessary information will be given to you.

Technique

A CBA question will probably give you one element of the statement to prepare, for instance, 'net cash flow from operating activities', 'capital expenditure' or 'financing'.

Make sure you know what items are included under each heading.

Advantages

- Business survival needs cash
- Cash flow is more objective than profit
- Creditors need to know if they will be paid
- More comparability between companies
- Better basis for decision making
- Easy to understand, prepare and audit

Disadvantages

The disadvantages of cash flow accounting are basically the advantages of accruals accounting, for example, cash flow does *not* match income and expenditure in the profit and loss account.

21: Internal and external audit

Topic List

Ownership v stewardship

External audit

Internal audit

Internal controls

Audit trail

You need to understand the differences between internal and external audit.

For the purposes of your exam, details of internal audit and internal controls are the most important topics. They are most likely to crop up in straightforward MCQs.

Ownership

The owners of a business may delegate the day to day running to a manager (eg with a limited company, the shareholders delegate to the directors).

The owners need to ensure that the stewardship of the business is being effectively carried out. This is the purpose of an audit.

Stewardship

The concept of stewardship embraces several functions.

- Ensuring the assets of the business are properly recorded, valued and insured
- Emphasising the need to control costs, improve efficiency and optimise profits, eg value for money audits
- Ensuring the maintenance and security of assets

Stewardship extends to all users of accounts, internal and external.

External auditors report to members, as an independent party, on whether the statutory accounts give a true and fair view. It is a legal requirement for companies as a result of the ownership/stewardship split.

External audit procedures are governed by the Auditing Practices Board (APB).

- Issues auditing standards and guidelines
- Has authority over external auditors so that audits must be carried out in accordance with such standards and guidelines

True and fair view

This term is not defined in company law or accounting standards. However it is taken to mean 'reasonably accurate and free from bias or distortion.'

Internal audit

Role: various, defined by management but may include the following.

- Review of accounting systems and controls
- Examination of financial/operating information
- VFM audit (economy, efficiency, effectiveness)
- Review of implementation of corporate policies
- Special investigations
- Investigations into allegations of fraud or misappropriation of assets

Essential elements

- Independence. The internal auditors will be employees, but should still be independent of the line management whose sphere of authority they may audit. They should report to the board or to a special internal audit committee and not to the finance director

- Appraisal. The internal auditors need unrestricted access to records, assets and personnel as they need to appraise the work of other people

- Staffing and training. The internal audit department (IAD) needs adequate skills to carry out its function and must be adequately staffed
- Relationships. Without threatening independence, the IAD must establish good working relationships with management, the external auditor and any audit committee
- Due care. Adequate standards of integrity and quality should be maintained
- Planning, controlling and recording
- Evidence. IAD should obtain sufficient, relevant and reliable evidence on which to base reasonable conclusions and recommendations
- Reporting. IAD should report its findings and recommendations promptly to an appropriate level of management

Internal auditors may carry out similar work to external auditors with some important differences:

- They are employees of the enterprise
- They report to management

Usually they report on controls which should exist in the enterprise or test balances in the management accounts

Internal controls

There are eight types of controls.

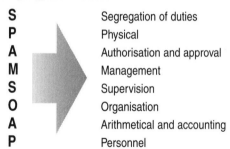

S	Segregation of duties
P	Physical
A	Authorisation and approval
M	Management
S	Supervision
O	Organisation
A	Arithmetical and accounting
P	Personnel

An operational system does *not* need to possess all of the SPAMSOAP controls.
In an exam question, you may need to indicate what is essential, what is desirable and what is optional.

Audit trail

This is a means by which an auditor can follow through a transaction from its origin to its ultimate location or vice versa

In a *manual accounting system* an audit trail consists of hard copy evidence of transactions, the relevant documents being preserved, eg purchase order, GRN, purchase advice.

In *computerised systems* (the majority) an audit trail is a record of file updating, enabling a trace to be kept of all operations on files. An audit trail may not be apparent in a computer system, for several reasons.

- Output may be a summary of items not individual transactions
- Records may be overwritten
- Reports may be on an exception basis only

However, adequate processing controls should enable an overall reconciliation of records/transactions input and processed to be made.

Fraud

The word fraud can be used to refer to irregularities involving the use of criminal deception to obtain an unjust or illegal advantage.

Common areas

- Ghost employees
- Miscasting of payroll
- Pocketing unclaimed wages
- Commission
- Altering cheques
- Initiating false expense claims
- Using company assets for personal gain
- Pocketing fully depreciated assets

Prevention

- Good system of internal control
- Surprise audits
- Personnel procedures
- Procedure manuals
- Segregation of duties

22: Interpreting company accounts

Topic List

Profitability and return on capital

Liquidity, gearing and working capital

This section looks at how we can read and interpret the financial statements. Ratios are tools which allow us to assess the figures presented.

This is a key area of the syllabus and you will take it forward to the next financial accounting papers.

Purpose

Analysis of a company's financial statements is performed by the following:

- Interested parties outside the business who are seeking to know more about the company (potential investors)
- Management wishing to interpret their company's past performance in order to make improvements for the future

Financial statements can be assessed using ratio analysis.

- Past trends of the same business (analysis through time) and compare to budget
- Comparative information for similar businesses (analysis by competitors)

Profitability

Return on capital employed:

$$\frac{\text{Profit on ordinary activities before interest and tax}}{\text{Capital employed}}$$

This ratio tells us how well total capital employed (equity and long-term debt) has been utilised. It judges profits earned in relation to the size of the business.

There are different ways of calculating ROCE. If the examiner tells you how to calculate it you should, of course, follow his instructions.

Return on equity:

$$\frac{\text{Profit after tax less preference dividends}}{\text{Shareholders' funds less preference shares}}$$

This indicates to ordinary shareholders how well their investment has performed.

Asset turnover: $\dfrac{\text{Turnover}}{\text{Total asset less current liabilities}}$

This shows the turnover that is generated from each £1 worth of asset employed. The higher the turnover per £1 invested, the more efficient the business.

Gross profit margin: $\dfrac{\text{Gross profit}}{\text{Turnover}} \times 100\%$

Net profit margin:

$$\frac{\text{Profit before interest and tax}}{\text{Turnover}} \times 100\%$$

A high net profit margin indicates the following:

- Costs are being controlled
- Sales prices are high compared to costs

Note: ROCE = asset turnover × net profit margin

Liquidity

Liquidity ratios give an indication as to whether or not a company will be able to meet its commitments as they fall due.

Current ratio: $\frac{\text{Current assets}}{\text{Current liabilities}}$

This ratio should be more than 1:1. It gives an indication of the company's margin of safety.

Quick ratio (acid test): $\frac{\text{Current assets less stock}}{\text{Current liabilities}}$

This ratio recognises that stock takes time to convert to cash. By excluding stock, the ratio is prudent.

Debtor days: $\frac{\text{Debtors}}{\text{Turnover}} \times 365$

This shows the average credit period taken by customers.

Stock turnover: $\frac{\text{Average stock held}}{\text{Cost of sales}} \times 365$

This shows the average period that stock is stored.

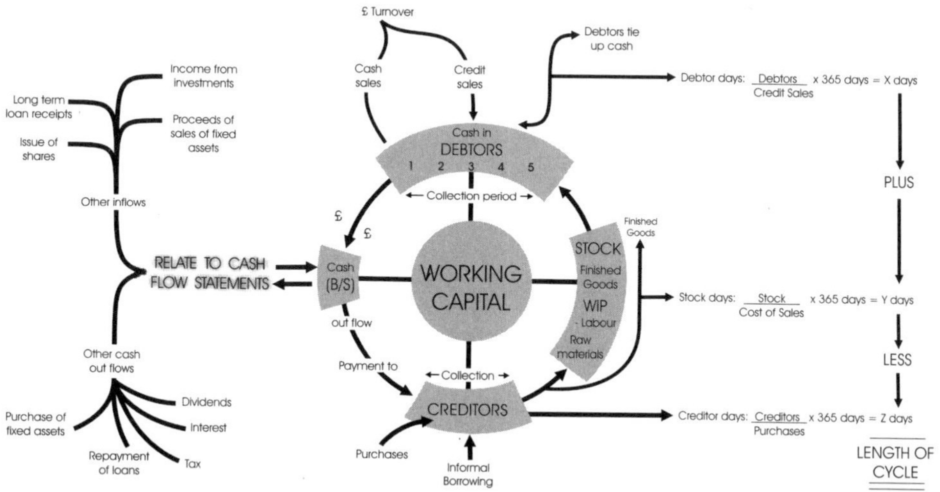
£ Turnover
Cash sales
Credit sales
Debtors tie up cash
Debtor days: Debtors / Credit Sales x 365 days = X days
Income from investments
Long term loan receipts
Proceeds of sales of fixed assets
Issue of shares
Cash in
DEBTORS
1 2 3 4 5
← Collection period →
Other inflows
PLUS
£
£
Finished Goods
STOCK
Finished Goods
WIP
- Labour
Raw materials
RELATE TO CASH FLOW STATEMENTS
Cash (B/S)
WORKING CAPITAL
Stock days: Stock / Cost of Sales x 365 days = Y days
out flow
Other cash out flows
Payment to
← Collection →
LESS
CREDITORS
Creditor days: Creditors / Purchases x 365 days = Z days
Dividends
Purchase of fixed assets
Interest
Repayment of loans
Tax
Purchases
Informal Borrowing
LENGTH OF CYCLE

Gearing

This is a way of comparing how much long-term finance is provided by 'equity' (ordinary shares and reserves) and how much is provided by 'prior charge' capital (debentures and preference shares).

Interest cover: $\dfrac{\text{Profit before interest and tax}}{\text{Interest charges}}$

This shows whether a company is earning enough profits before interest and tax to pay its interest costs comfortably.

Gearing: $\dfrac{\text{Prior charge capital (loans + preference shares)}}{\text{Shareholders' funds (ord. share capital + all reserves)}}$

This looks at the ratio of prior charge capital to equity.

A higher ratio indicates greater risk to shareholders.

Notes

Notes

Notes

Notes